D0359279

Never Turn Back

Father Serra's Mission

Never Turn Back
Father Serra's Mission

by Jim Rawls
Alex Haley, General Editor

Illustrations by George Guzzi

STECK-VAUGHN
C O M P A N Y
A Subsidiary of National Education Corporation

Published by Steck-Vaughn Company.

Text, illustrations, and cover art copyright © 1993 by Dialogue Systems, Inc., 627 Broadway, New York, New York, 10012.

Cover art by George Guzzi

Printed in China
11 788 05

Library of Congress Cataloging-in-Publication Data
Rawls, James J.
    Never turn back : Father Serra's mission / by James J. Rawls ; illustrated by George Guzzi.
      p.   cm. — (Stories of America)
    Summary: Describes the life of the Spanish priest who established missions in California in the late eighteenth century and discusses the lack of understanding between him and the Indians he came to convert.
    ISBN 0-8114-7221-3. — ISBN 0-8114-8061-5 (pbk.)
    1. Serra, Junípero, 1713-1784—Juvenile literature.
2. Diegueño Indians—Missions—Juvenile literature.
3. Missionaries—California—Biography—Juvenile literature. 4. Missionaries—Spain—Biography—Juvenile literature. [1. Serra, Junípero, 1713-1784. 2. Missionaries. 3. Diegueño Indians—Missions. 4. Indians of North America—California—Missions. 5. California—History— To 1846.] I. Guzzi, George, ill. II. Title, III. Series.
E99.D5S377   1993
979.4'02'092—dc20
[B]   92-12814
                                               CIP
                                             AC

ISBN 0-8114-7221-3 (Hardcover)

ISBN 0-8114-8061-5 (Softcover)

To Linda Chisholm and all those who share her commitment to the art of teaching.

Introduction
by Alex Haley, General Editor

Gold, Glory, and God. In school I learned how the three G's launched the ships of empire. Gold, Glory, and God brought the Spanish (and other Europeans, but the Spanish first and most spectacularly) to the Americas. Gold and glory came to Cortés and Pizarro with the bloody conquests of the Aztec and Mayan empires.

The conquerors were not alone. With them came missionaries who spread Christianity like a blanket over the defeated Indian populations. The missionaries came with extraordinary zeal. They came after the conquerors stopped coming. They came with those who built small settlements to claim American Indian lands for Spain so that other Europeans would not claim those same lands for England, France, or Russia. The best of them had sympathy, as Jim Rawls writes in his afterword, but not understanding.

Father Serra was one of the best of them. People feel strongly about Serra. Some are sure he is a hero, a saint. Others are sure that he is a villain, a destroyer of a people and their culture. His story shows how tangled are the roots of our history. His story shows the importance of understanding and how much is lost in its absence.

Contents

1 *Beginnings*

The old sandstone mission of San Xavier cast a long shadow over the dry, hard-packed soil of Baja California. Just within the mission's sun-stretched shadow stood two gray-robed Spanish padres. Their excited voices echoed off the mission's walls. Their laughter filled the air. Overhead, a pair of swallows, frightened by the laughter, burst into flight from atop the mission's tiled roof.

It was early morning on the first day of April 1769. The two priests were the best of friends. They had known each other for nearly thirty years. In that time they had shared many adventures together—adventures that made laughter and understanding between them easy. But this morning their laughter was edged with sadness. The two old friends were parting.

The older of the two was a small man, only five feet two inches tall. His name was Father Junípero Serra, and he looked even older than his fifty-five years. His face was deeply lined and sun-darkened. His body was battered by years of traveling and living in the wilderness. A slight wheezing sound came from his chest with each breath. His left leg, swollen and sore from an old injury that never seemed to heal, began to bother Serra. He stepped gingerly into the sunlight knowing the heat from the morning sun would gently warm his injured leg. His friend followed him, talking. Serra's dark eyes narrowed with sympathy as he listened to his companion. His friend spoke so earnestly—and so persistently.

Father Francisco Palóu was nine years younger than Serra. Long ago in Spain, he had been Father Serra's student. And what was once the respect of a student for his teacher had since grown into the deep affection of friendship.

Father Palóu had been up half the night trying to convince Father Serra to change his mind. Serra was determined to lead an expedition north to start Spain's first missions in Alta California. Palóu worried that the expedition would be too much for his friend.

He felt Serra was too old for such a journey. Palóu argued, your leg is bad and your health poor. There are mountains and deserts to cross. It is an impossible journey. You will only be foolishly risking your life.

But Serra only laughed. It wasn't a rude or thoughtless laugh. Serra was too fond of Palóu for that. He wanted Palóu to stop worrying. His laugh was meant to show that there was nothing to worry about. The journey wouldn't be *that* bad. He'd made worse. Besides, God would protect him. For Serra believed he was doing God's work. And surely no risk on God's behalf could be foolish.

After a pause, Serra looked at the still dawning sun. It spread the mission's shadow farther and farther from its walls. Time was escaping. He must leave soon. Palóu, too, knew that time was running out. This was his last chance to change Serra's mind.

Clearly, Serra cared nothing for his own well-being. Palóu must try some other way to convince him not to go. He told Serra that his injured leg would prevent him from keeping up with the others. This, Palóu warned, might bring disaster on the whole expedition. Serra might risk his life, thought Palóu, but would he want to risk the success of the expedition?

But Serra had made up his mind and would not unmake it now. "Let us not speak of that," he replied firmly. Then in a voice both deep and soft, he added, "I have placed all my confidence in God. I trust that He will grant me the strength to reach not only San Diego, to raise the Holy Cross, but also Monterey."

There was nothing for Palóu to do now but say goodbye to his old friend. He watched as Serra was helped onto his mule. Serra held his bad leg stiffly out as he settled into the saddle. The mule, as broken-down as its rider, brayed in complaint at this new burden.

"Goodbye, Francisco," Serra called, "until we meet in Monterey."

Father Palóu doubted such a meeting would ever take place. He feared that he would never see his friend again. "Goodbye, Junípero," he answered, "until eternity."

Then the two friends parted. The worn-out mule and the aging padre set out on the long journey to Alta California. In their wake trailed two servants. A pale dust cloud kicked up behind them. Palóu watched them melt into the distance.

As Junípero Serra's mule carried him along the rough trail, the old padre thought over the warnings of Father Palóu. He knew his dear friend meant well. But surely Father Palóu was being too cautious. Serra was positive God would bless his mission.

As if to confirm Serra's view, the first part of the journey passed easily enough. The two young servants helped with the cooking and care of the mules. At the end of each day's journey of twenty miles, they stopped to stay the night at one of the Spanish missions in Baja California.

After a week on the trail, Serra found himself thinking of days long past, when he was a boy in the little Spanish village of Petra. He recalled the happy times when he had played among the orchards of giant fig trees. He thought of the creaking windmills turning slowly in the sleepy afternoon breeze.

He remembered the grand old church of San Bernardino that stood near his boyhood home. He recalled kneeling in the candlelit shadow of the church's high altar. He could hear the beautiful, soft chanting of the priests celebrating the mass.

At fifteen, still a boy, Serra left Petra for the nearby city of Palma. There he began to study for the priesthood. And it was in Palma that he first heard the exciting stories of missionaries who had gone to faraway lands to spread their faith to others.

He heard of Francisco Solano. Solano had gone to South America with the Spanish conquerers. He converted to Christianity thousands and thousands of the Indians of Peru, Chile, and Argentina. For his work as a missionary, Solano was named a saint by the Catholic Church.

The stories about Solano and the other great missionaries fired Serra's young imagination. This, too, was what he wanted. He would bring his faith to a land where it had never been, teach his religion to a people who had never heard of it before.

Serra was ordained a priest and assigned to teach philosophy to young students studying for the priesthood. One of these was Francisco Palóu.

Father Serra was a very popular teacher. Yet somehow he was not satisfied. He couldn't get the stories of Solano and the other missionaries out of his mind. What he wanted was to be a missionary.

One afternoon, he went to visit his former student Father Palóu with a great secret. He was leaving Spain for North America. He was going to be a missionary among the Indians of North America. Nothing else would satisfy him and he knew it. Still, Serra did not want to go alone. Perhaps if he could explain himself well enough, share his enthusiasm and sense of mission, perhaps then Father Palóu might agree to come with him.

Serra searched for words to explain his visit. He mumbled something about making a decision. Then to his surprise, Palóu interrupted, blurting out that *he* had made a great decision, too. He had decided to become a missionary!

"What do you think?" Palóu asked.

For a moment there was no answer. Serra could hardly believe his ears. Then he quickly told Palóu of his own decision.

"I have been praying," Serra concluded, "that God would stir the heart of someone to go with me. And now my prayers have been answered."

The two friends left Spain in August of 1749. They sailed as missionaries to the great Spanish colony of New Spain. After a difficult voyage, they landed in December at Vera Cruz on the east coast of New Spain.

From there they walked 250 miles to Mexico City, once the capital of the Aztec empire and now the capital of the Spanish empire in North America. The road they traveled was a rough dirt track that passed through tropical forests and empty deserts.

The heat and *zancudos*—mosquitoes—attacked the two travelers without mercy. Serra scratched at his many bites, one of which became infected. First his left foot and then nearly the whole leg began to bleed and swell. This little bite became the injury that plagued him the rest of his life.

On January 1, 1750, two weeks after they began their walk, Serra and Palóu arrived at the College of San Fernando in Mexico City.

There they joined San Fernando's community of 114 priests. They tended the college's orchards and fields. They prayed alone in tiny, dimly lit rooms and together in the great church with the rest of the community. In between, they studied, thought, and prepared for missionary work.

One day, San Fernando's director called all the priests together. He told them about the missions in Sierra Gorda. Things were going very badly there. Sickness had just claimed the lives of four priests. If the priests weren't replaced immediately, these missions would fail. "Now," he concluded, "who of you will volunteer for the Sierra Gorda?"

Serra had only been at San Fernando a short while. Others had more preparation. Others had more experience. But no one was as ready. He was the first to speak up. "Here I am; send me!" From his student days, Serra longed for this moment. This was how he had chosen to serve God, and now the chance to do so was before him. And he seized it.

Soon a dozen voices echoed Serra's. The pleased director chose six to go to Sierra Gorda, including both Serra and Palóu.

Father Serra thrived in the rugged mountains so distant from Mexico City. He worked tirelessly in the harsh mountain air. He learned the Pame Indian language from a Mexican boy who had been raised by the Pame. He staged plays and processions to attract the Pame to church and preached to them with all his heart. He worked in the fields with Palóu and the Pame. He brought oxen and sheep and goats from San Fernando to the mountains.

The barren fields began to prosper and soon there was enough food not only to support the mission communities but also to sell in the nearby mining towns. The Sierra Gorda missions were a success.

In 1767 Father Serra was rewarded for his work by being named *presidente* of all the missions in Baja California. Serra accepted the post but one part of his dream was yet incomplete. What he most wanted was to build new missions of his own.

He pleaded with José de Galvéz, the king's deputy in Mexico City, to allow him to lead an expedition into Alta California. No missionaries had ever been there. Like Solano, he could be the first.

For Serra, this dream came true in 1768, only a year later, when he was asked to lead an expedition north. The king wanted missions begun along the bays of San Diego and Monterey in Alta California.

The forts that protected these missions and the missions themselves could help make Spain's claim on this land permanent. The British and the Russians were said to be planning to seize the area for themselves. If the Spanish didn't hurry, they might lose this distant land.

Serra cared little about the plans of Russia and Britain. He cared only about pursuing his dream. His one regret was that Palóu, who had followed him to Baja California, was not coming with him. Palóu would remain at San Xavier mission. He would take Serra's place as *presidente* of the Baja missions. Serra was happy for his friend, but happier for himself.

2 *In Their Own Land*

For over a month, Junípero Serra and his two servants worked their way north through Baja California. In all, they covered over five hundred miles that month. At each of the Baja missions, Serra was greeted warmly by the padres. Some had known him in Mexico City; others knew him only as their *presidente*. But each was pleased to have a visitor.

The missions of Baja California were lonely outposts on the far northwestern rim of the Spanish empire. The dry climate and sandy soil of the peninsula made farming difficult. The missions were often desperately short of supplies. As Father Serra traveled north, he did his best to encourage the struggling missionaries.

The last of the Baja missions was Santa María. Here Serra would meet up with the military leader of the expedition to Alta California, Gaspar de Portolá. Captain Portolá was ten years younger than Serra. He was a pleasant man, a careful man, and every inch a soldier. These qualities made him a good officer for Serra to work with. They also made him the right person to command the twenty-five leather-jacketed soldiers; thirty Christian Indians; and the assortment of muleteers, cooks, and servants that made up the rest of the expedition.

On the eleventh of May 1769, the expedition began its march north. Serra's joy was complete. At last he was on his way to a land where no other Christian missionaries had been before.

"I praised the Lord," wrote Serra in his diary, "giving thanks to His Divine Majesty that

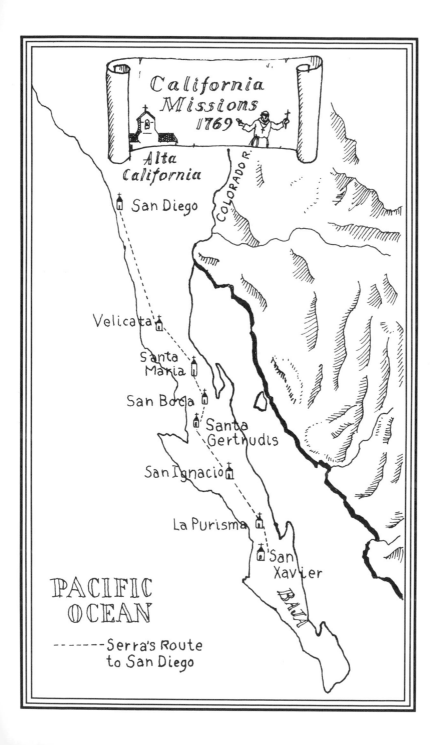

after desiring this for so many years, He granted me the favor of being among the pagans in their own land."

Serra's good fortune, however, had not included a cure for his injured leg. Instead, the ride to Santa María had greatly aggravated it. As they rode north, it began to swell again. The wound was inflamed and the pain was great enough to make riding or walking difficult. The warnings of Palóu suddenly nagged at Serra's conscience.

Captain Portolá learned of Serra's condition and became alarmed. He worried that if Serra's leg got any worse, he would slow the expedition down. As it was, Portolá knew that even if things went well, their supplies would barely last the length of the trip. Who knew what might happen if there were any delays?

The captain watched Serra for the first week of their march north. Finally, he decided he must try to convince the padre to return to Santa María.

"Padre *Presidente,*" he began carefully, wanting not to offend the proud padre. "Your

Reverence is aware that you are unable to follow the expedition. We are only a short distance from our starting place."

Serra listened with some impatience. Yes, he and his servants had fallen behind the main line of marchers. This was obvious. But he would catch up when his leg felt better.

"If Your Reverence desires," Portolá politely persisted, "I will have you carried back to Santa María. There you can recuperate, and we will continue our journey."

But Serra gave the captain the same reply he gave Palóu. "God will give me the strength to reach San Diego, as He has given me the strength to come so far."

Serra was resolved. Portolá was not. He asked the padre what would happen in case God did not give him the strength to continue.

"In case He does not," Serra answered crisply, "I will conform myself to His most holy will. Even though I should die on the way, *I shall not turn back.*"

Portolá realized it was hopeless. If Serra insisted on continuing, then he would have to be carried. He ordered the Christian Indians to make a stretcher for the padre.

Serra wanted to protest but knew it would be a mistake. The idea of being a burden to the Christian Indians embarrassed him. However, unless they carried him, Portolá would not let him go on. This was the only way. Still, it pained him, and he had to wonder if it was faith or pride that made him so determined.

That afternoon, Father Serra called one of the young muleteers to him. He asked the startled muleteer if he knew of a remedy for his injured leg.

"Why, Father, what remedy could I know of? Do you think I am a surgeon? I'm a muleteer. I've healed only the sores of animals."

"Well then, son," Serra replied, "just imagine that I am an animal and that this wound is the sore of an animal. Make me the same remedy which you would apply to a mule."

The boy must have wondered if the old padre was crazy. He looked at him for a long while. "Father," he said finally, "I shall do so in order to please you."

The muleteer mixed together some tallow and green herbs. He warmed them over a flame. Then he carefully applied the mixture to Serra's wound.

That night Serra slept soundly. By the next morning, he was much improved. The boy's remedy had worked! Serra told Captain Portolá that a stretcher would not be needed. He could ride his mule or walk as he pleased, and he could do either without delaying the expedition.

So for the next six weeks, the party advanced north. They crossed dry, desert arroyos and high mountains. As they moved on through the month of June, the land gradually became more pleasing, less forbidding. They passed groves of cottonwoods and streams of sparkling water. They rested near vines of wild grapes and bushes covered with pink rose blossoms.

Nearing San Diego, the expedition came across several large Indian villages. The villagers were Tipais, which means "the people." Their area of settlement covered the southern edge of Alta California and the northern tip of Baja California.

The people of the villages watched these strange men approaching. The leather jackets, heavy cloth shirts, and pantaloons were indeed curiosities. The Spanish themselves were less impressive than their strange costumes. Food supplies were low, and the men all looked sick and weak from the weeks of travel.

A group of Tipais approached the Spanish one morning. They carried baskets of fish freshly taken from nearby streams. The Spanish called for their translator. He was a Christian Indian brought from the San Xavier mission. Unfortunately for Serra and Portolá, his native language was competely different from that of the Tipais. He understood no more of what the Tipais said than the Spanish did.

Instead, the two groups of strangers spoke with hand gestures and pantomime. The Spanish were surprised at how much interest the Tipais had in Spanish cloth. They brought the fish to trade for cloth.

At first, the Spanish tried to trade only small pieces of cloth to the Tipais, one small piece for each fish. But the Tipais refused. Their baskets contained large fish as well as small ones. They would trade small fish for small cloth pieces. If the Spanish wanted the bigger fish, they'd have to trade bigger pieces of cloth. The Spanish were too hungry to quibble further. They completed the trading on the Tipais' terms.

A few days south of San Diego Bay, the Spanish encountered another Tipai village. Seeing all these villages so close to his destination pleased Serra. The mission planned for San Diego would seek to draw its converts from villages like these. Best of all, this was the largest village they had yet seen. Serra, hoping he might have the success of his boyhood hero, named the place after the missionary Francisco Solano.

While they visited among the villagers, Serra was struck by the people's friendliness and warmth. One group came and sat in a circle around him. A mother placed her baby girl in Serra's arms, which brought a smile to the padre's round, dark face.

The baby twisted and squirmed in the priest's arms. More than anything, Serra ached to baptize the baby, to make her a member of the Catholic Church.

This, though, he couldn't do without also founding a mission here. Without a mission, who would see to the baby's religious instruction? Where would she go to church? Who would instruct the baby's parents in the teachings of the Catholic faith? Who would teach them the ways of the Spanish? A mission needs priests for these things.

And it needs soldiers. Who else would keep the Indians from running back to their villages and their traditional ways?

As Serra left the village, he made the sign of the cross over the Tipais, blessing them. He longed to reach his destination. The first mission would be along the bay at San Diego, not here. That had been decided. Serra would have to wait until San Diego.

Early on the morning of July 1, Father Serra caught his first glimpse of the bay of San

Diego. Sea birds rode the swirling air currents, gliding and dipping over the Pacific waves. Serra felt a rush of joy as he watched. He spotted two supply ships riding silently at anchor in the bay. There was relief for the weary, hungry expedition!

It took them all morning to work their way down to the beach. But by one o'clock, he felt the warm, moist sand beneath his feet. "THANKS BE TO GOD," wrote Serra in his diary.

Father Serra had good reason to be thankful. He had traveled more than nine hundred miles from San Xavier to San Diego. He was eight thousand miles from his boyhood home in Spain. But Serra was no longer thinking about the past. His mind was filled with thoughts of the work that lay ahead.

3 *But None Would Stay*

Serra thought San Diego a wonderful location for a mission. Its wide grassy plains would make good pasturelands. The San Diego River offered a rich supply of fresh water. Along the river grew willow, poplar, and sycamore trees. These would provide fuel for cooking and timber for construction.

The land itself was very fertile. Wild grapes, roses, and asparagus grew everywhere. The plains and hills were alive with deer and antelope, quail and rabbits.

Most important of all to Father Serra, the area around San Diego had a large Indian population. Like the Indians to the south, these were Tipais. No one in Serra's party spoke their language or understood their customs. This would make things harder, but Serra had become a missionary because it was a hard road, not an easy one. His heart beat with the joy of anticipation.

Serra's joy was short-lived. An advance party from his own expedition was there to greet them. They had arrived a month earlier but suffered greatly on their trip north. Food supplies had run out. Sickness and exhaustion kept the men from hunting or fishing. Instead, they had grown sicker and weaker. Some had even died from hunger.

Puzzled, Serra looked out to sea. He could see the two supply ships, the *San Antonio* and the *San Carlos,* riding at anchor. Why hadn't they helped? But the news from the ships was even worse.

They had sailed north from San Blas, a colonial port on the western coast of New Spain. The *San Antonio* had been lucky. Its voyage had lasted only 54 days. But the *San Carlos* had been blown off course. After 110 days at sea, its crew had arrived in San Diego more dead than alive. No one on board was well enough to even lower a boat. Twenty-one sailors on the two ships had died from scurvy.

Serra and Portolá had their hands full. There were sick and dying Spaniards on shore and aboard the ships.

After the sick had been attended to, Captain Portolá held an emergency meeting. He announced that the *San Antonio* would return to San Blas for fresh supplies. Serra would remain here to get the San Diego mission underway while Portolá led the bulk of the expedition north to locate Monterey Bay, the site of the second mission.

The Tipais watched the intruders from a distance. They saw the Christian Indians and the few healthy soldiers work, gathering brush to build huts. One hut was made larger than the others. They saw Serra and others tending the many sick among the intruders. These strangers seemed a weak people.

Serra was aware that the Tipais were watching. He was eager to begin his missionary work. While he worked, he planned the ceremony that would begin the San Diego mission. It would be rich in pomp and color to impress the Tipais.

On the morning of July 16, Father Serra was ready. He led a solemn procession to the larger hut. Serra wore a fine white linen robe. A short cape of brightly colored silk decorated his shoulders. Behind him came a group of soldiers carrying a large wooden cross. They raised the cross in front of the hut. Father Serra sprinkled holy water on this temporary church. He named the new mission San Diego de Alcalá.

Father Serra then led the procession inside. He sang a High Mass and preached a sermon. He prayed for a rich "harvest of souls" among the Tipais. "May God give them His grace so that in a short time all will become Christians."

Outside, the soldiers fired their muskets in repeated volleys. Puffs of gunsmoke passed like incense before the cross.

That evening Father Serra opened a large leather-bound book. Its pages were all blank. At the top of the first page he wrote the name of the mission and the date of its founding. He prepared the pages for names of Christian converts. He left space to record baptisms, marriages, and burials.

But the weeks of late July and early August went by with no names to record in the mission book. Serra began to wonder if he would ever be able to fill these pages. A few Tipais came to visit, but none would stay.

Even more troubling to Serra were the many Tipais in the nearby villages who refused to come anywhere near the mission. They had heard how many of the intruders had died of a strange and awful disease. When the small man in the gray robe tried to lure them with modest gifts of food, they backed away. They feared that it was the food the intruders ate that made them sick.

Serra did not understand why they backed away from him. With great difficulty, he tried to explain his purpose in coming to their land. He spoke to them in Spanish and made signs in the air with his hands.

He told them he wanted them to come and live at the mission. They would learn to become Christians.

He explained how they would be expected to stay at the mission the rest of their lives. They would need to learn prayers and the customs of the church. At the mission they would be taught to support the community by becoming farmers, carpenters, and blacksmiths. They would learn a new religion and a new way of life.

The Tipais had little interest in what Father Serra had to say. They saw no need to learn what he wanted to teach. They had lived in California for thousands of years. They already knew how to use the resources of this rich and beautiful land.

As a people, they moved with the seasons, gathering the different foods provided by the Earth Mother. Each spring, they hunted small game in the coastal canyons and lower foothills. In the early summer they dried ripening cactus fruits for winter storage. In July and August, they moved higher into the hills to gather seeds, wild plums, and other fruits. In the fall, they gathered acorns and piñon nuts.

Always they followed the Earth Mother's trail of gifts. Why should they stay in one place for all time? Why should they live like these sickly intruders?

Serra understood none of this. Nor did he understand that the Tipais had their own religion. Their priests, or shamans, taught the people about the creation of the world and all living things. They told stories of the creator gods, Earth Mother and Primal Water. The shamans were powerful teachers and healers. If the Spanish shamans were as powerful, why were their people so sickly?

The only thing that the Spanish had that seemed to interest the Tipais was their clothing and cloth. Like their cousins to the south, these Tipais were fascinated by cloth materials.

One night, soldiers aboard the *San Carlos* discovered several Tipais cutting cloth from the ship's sail. The angry soldiers fired their muskets to warn the Tipais away. Unaware of how dangerous the muskets were, the Tipais laughed at the Spanish as they retreated with their strips of cloth. Some stopped to imitate the barking of the muskets.

This was one of several small conflicts between the two peoples. By the middle of August, the Tipais were weary of these intruders. Perhaps they had thought that Serra's small party would leave as had the larger group of men that had come with them. But they had not. Instead, they lingered on. New huts were built. The sickly strangers were growing well.

For the Tipais, it was time to move up into the hills to begin gathering wild plums and other ripening fruits. Before they went, they decided to rid their land of these bothersome strangers. Portolá had left only a handful of soldiers to protect the San Diego mission. It would not take many warriors to get rid of them.

4 *Harvest of Souls*

Father Serra stood at the doorway of his brush hut on the morning of August 15, 1769. He had just said Mass for his tiny congregation of soldiers and Christian Indians. He watched as four soldiers who had attended the service walked toward the beach. Others drifted back to their huts or to their duties.

As he turned to enter his hut, Serra was startled by the soft drumming of footsteps. Gathering around the mission were twenty or more Tipais. The padre smiled and began to greet them. The smile froze on his face. The Tipais were armed. They were carrying bows and arrows. Some had daggers in hand. Others held heavy clubs of curved wood.

There was a pause that seemed endless. Then came a sudden yell that brought the four soldiers running back from the beach. The Tipais charged toward the mission. Father Serra ran for cover.

The soldiers went scurrying for their leather jackets and muskets. Arrows came raining down from the sky. The Spanish fired their muskets, sending deadly shot toward the Tipais.

The mission blacksmith ran shouting among the soldiers. He urged the soldiers on, "Long live the faith of Jesus Christ."

Serra didn't want the Tipais killed in the name of Jesus. He fell to his knees and prayed. He asked God that no one be killed in the battle that raged outside his hut.

But several Tipais already lay dead as Serra prayed. The missionary's prayers were interrupted when his young servant fell through the curtained door of the padre's hut. The servant howled in pain, his hands clawing at his throat. An arrow had pierced his neck. "Father, absolve

me," he whispered, "for the Indians have killed me."

The gunfire outside continued. More Tipais fell dead or wounded. Before long, the Tipais saw that it was pointless to press the attack against the Spanish muskets. Carrying their dead and wounded, they returned to their villages.

Father Serra stood again at the doorway of his hut. The smoke of battle hung over the mission. Arrows littered the ground. The blacksmith and two soldiers lay wounded. Serra's face showed the pain he felt in his heart. Is this why I have come so far, he wondered. How can I ever make Christians of a people such as these? Will any of them come near the mission again?

The mission soldiers also wondered if the Tipais would return. If they did, the soldiers wanted to be ready. They built a wooden stockade around the mission huts. Guards were posted at the stockade gate.

In the days that followed, a few of the Tipais did come to the mission. They came seeking help for their wounded. The Spanish muskets had given the weak mission soldiers special powers. Perhaps they had other powers that might help heal as well as they killed.

One of the Tipais who came was a fifteen-year-old boy. He wanted to learn more about the Spanish. Unlike the other Tipais, he accepted the food offered by the Spanish. He even learned a few Spanish words.

Father Serra saw in the boy a chance to reach the other Tipais. He told the boy how pleased he would be if he could bring a small child to the mission to be baptized. Serra explained that pouring water on the child's brow would make the baby a child of God. Serra promised the baby a special gift of clothing.

A few days later, the boy returned. With him came a small crowd that included a young family with a baby boy. Serra could barely contain his excitement. This would be his first baptism at the new mission—the first in Alta California. At last he would have a name to write in the mission record book.

Serra presented the child with some clothing. The baby's parents eagerly accepted the gift. Serra gently placed the baby in the crook of his left arm and began the baptism.

A group of soldiers gathered nearby, keeping nervous eyes on Serra and the Tipais. Serra read the prayers of baptism. He placed a little oil on the baby's chest and forehead. The boy's parents watched each gesture closely.

Finally Father Serra lifted a shell containing holy water. He tipped it over the baby's head. Water splashed down and a look of horror crossed the face of the baby's father.

He grabbed the baby from Serra's grasp and ran from the mission. The boy's father was outraged. Was the gray-robed man trying to drown his son? He held his son tightly to his chest and was gone. The other Tipais followed him.

Several of the soldiers readied their muskets. Others began to chase the retreating Tipais. Serra stopped them. He told the soldiers to let them go. Overcome with sorrow, the padre watched until the Tipais disappeared from sight. His eyes filled with tears.

Later that day, Father Serra walked in silence along the beach. Up ahead was a half-buried log of driftwood. There he sat and rested, stretching his injured leg on the wood's warm surface. He watched as waves curled and broke with a roar on the sandy beach. Gulls skimmed low over the churning surf.

Father Serra turned and gazed at the low hills that ringed the bay. In the distance he saw slender columns of gray smoke. They rose in wind-bent lines from the nearby Tipai villages.

Questions flooded Serra's mind. Why had the Tipais attacked the mission? Why had they run from the baptism? Try as he might, Serra could find no answers.

He closed his eyes and sighed deeply. He thought of the stories he had heard long ago of missionaries in faraway lands. He recalled that they had all faced great problems before they succeeded. They had had to overcome doubt and early failure—sometimes, many failures. But they hadn't given up. Neither would he.

Father Serra stood and brushed sand from

his robe. He began walking toward the mission. San Diego de Alacalá, he promised, would be a success. It would be a success whatever the price.

And it would be only the beginning. When Portolá returned, they would start work on the founding of the second mission at Monterey. Together they would provide God a rich harvest of souls.

Epilogue

Five years after the founding of San Diego de Alcalá, Junípero Serra was once again joined in his work by his friend, Francisco Palóu. When Serra died in California in 1784, Palóu took his place as *presidente* of the Alta California missions. Eventually, twenty-one missions dotted the California coast, stretching from San Diego to San Francisco. They marked the beginning of Spanish settlement in California.

After Serra's death, Palóu wrote a biography of his friend. Palóu's book and the papers of Father Serra provided much of the information for the story you just read. Unfortunately, as

useful as they are, they don't tell us the whole story. For instance, they don't tell us what happened to the baby Father Serra tried to baptize. They don't tell us his name or the names of his parents. That information is lost to us.

We do know, however, that the missions also marked the beginning of a long and tragic decline for the California Indian peoples. Their way of life was attacked by the mission fathers. It was attacked even by those, like Father Serra, who had sympathy for the Indians but lacked an understanding of their ways.

The missions also brought European diseases to California—diseases that the Indians had never experienced before. Confined in the missions, the Indians of California caught these diseases, grew sick, and died by the thousands. In all likelihood, the baby and his family were among those thousands who died. This awful fact, too, is part of Father Serra's story.

Afterword

The people and events in this story are real. Some ordinary details—swallows lifting off from a roof, the way Serra fussed with his injured leg, the braying of a weary mule—are made up. But anything we have added is consistent with what we know of the people, land, and customs of the time. Nothing of importance has been changed. All of the conversations that appear within quotation marks are the actual words—translated, of course—recorded from Serra's time.

Notes

Page 1 The Spanish founded the first mission in Baja (or Lower) California in 1697. Over the next 70 years, more than 600 Spanish missionaries worked on the narrow peninsula. They established 16 missions and baptized thousands of Baja Indians. Both Father Serra and Father Palóu were deeply concerned about the spread of new diseases among the mission Indians of the area. "If it goes on at this rate," Father Palóu noted at the time, "in a short time Baja California will come to an end."

Page 6 The expedition to Alta (or Upper) California included two additional parties to the one led by Serra. One was an advance party that preceded Serra's group up the Baja peninsula. The other consisted of two supply ships sent along the Pacific Coast to meet the overland parties in San Diego.

Page 7 Father Serra was born on November 24, 1713. His boyhood home in the village of Petra was a simple one. The living quarters had rough wooden floors, plain furniture, and the dim light of an oil-burning lamp. In later years, he would ask, "What more do we want than a little tortilla and the wild herbs of the field?"

Page 9 New Spain was the largest of Spain's colonies in North and South America. It included all of present-day Mexico and most of the southwestern states of the present-day United States. In 1700, more than 100,000 people lived in its capital, Mexico City.

Page 11 Even today, the Sierra Gorda is a rugged, forbidding land where few people live. It is located in the heart of the Sierra Madre range. These mountains extend from north to south, between the Atlantic Ocean and Mexico's central plateau.

Page 11 The Pames grew corn, beans, and pumpkins. They also traded palm mats and sisal ropes for cotton. From the cotton the Pames wove cloth and made garments.

Page 12 José de Galvéz was a strange man. He was hard working, intelligent, and well organized, but he was also vain, selfish, and more than a little unstable. Some historians even believe that he may have suffered from temporary attacks of insanity. He once proposed importing six hundred apes from the jungles of Guatemala. It was Galvéz's idea that the apes might be used as soldiers to fight the Indians of northern Mexico.

Page 15 Like Father Serra, Captain Portolá volunteered to serve as a leader of the expedition to Alta California. He had been a military leader in Italy and Portugal before coming to New Spain. He also had served as governor of Baja California since 1767.

Page 21 Within the borders of modern-day California, there were at least five major Native American language groups, and as many as twenty-one distinct languages. The people of the region around San Diego were of the Yuman culture, which included, among others, the Ipai and Tipai tribal groups. Once the missions were established, the Spanish renamed the mission Indians after the mission. The Tipai and Ipai were called the Diegueños, after the San Diego mission.

Page 24 Soldiers were an essential part of the mission community. Posted to a land they described as *este último rincón del mundo,* "the last corner of the earth," these tough peasant soldiers were responsible for mission discipline. Mission Indians were subjected to a rigid work and instruction schedule. There were many rules. One of the most important rules was that once attached to a mission, the Indians were not allowed to leave without permission from the padres.

Failures to obey the rules or to learn their lessons were often punishable by floggings with leather whips or imprisonment in wooden stocks or iron shackles. Such harsh punishments were common tools of discipline and "instruction" throughout Europe at the time. The brutality of the punishments varied, depending on the personalities and circumstances of those inflicting them. Soldiers banished to "the last corner of the earth" were not likely to be gentled by their hard existence nor to be sympathetic to a people they saw as pagan savages.

Page 28 Scurvy is a painful and potentially deadly disease caused by the lack of vitamin C in one's diet. Sailors in the 1700s often suffered from scurvy because their diets on ocean voyages lacked fresh fruits and vegetables. A ship on a voyage that lasted as long as the *San Carlos*'s could lose most of its crew to scurvy. People with scurvy bleed easily, particularly around their teeth and gums, lose their appetite, and, if they are sick or injured, heal very slowly, if at all.

Page 29 The details of the ceremony founding the San Diego mission were taken from Serra's own descriptions of the founding of this and other missions in Alta California.

Page 32 We have no record of the Tipais' thoughts. We do know from Spanish records that the Tipai offered the most determined resistance to Spanish missionary life. Thoughts and motivations provided here are our best guesses of what lay behind their interactions with the Spanish.

Pages 35–36 These were the traditional weapons of the Tipais and were probably the ones used on this occasion. Later, the Tipais obtained guns and horses from the Spanish.

Page 40 Again, we don't know why the father of the Tipai infant grabbed his son away at that moment in the ceremony. We can only assume that something about it either offended him or suggested that it might be harmful to his son.

Page 41 Father Serra never forgot this small incident. Often over the course of his life, he would recall this day, telling this story while his eyes filled with tears.

Jim Rawls lives in California and teaches at Diablo Valley College. In addition to *Never Turn Back* and *Dame Shirley and the Gold Rush,* Mr. Rawls is the author of a number of scholarly works.